D1285786

J 363.7 KOPP

Kopp, Megan

Be the change for the environment

WITHDRAWN

HUDSON PUBLIC LIBRARY
3 WASHINGTON STREET
@ WOOD SQUARE
HUDSON, MA 01749

BE THE CHANGE

for the Environment

Megan Kopp

Crabtree Publishing Company
www.crabtreebooks.com

JUL 1 5 2015

Dedicated by Samara Parent

For Elliott and Nathan, you can be the change!

Author
Megan Kopp

Publishing plan research and development
Reagan Miller

Editor
Anastasia Suen

Proofreader and indexer
Wendy Scavuzzo

Design
Samara Parent

Photo research
Samara Parent

Production coordinator and prepress technician
Samara Parent

Print coordinator
Katherine Berti

Photographs
Dreamstime: p. 7 (bottom)
Earth Saver Girl - Brooklyn Wright p. 8, 9
istockphoto: (front cover)
Thinkstock: p. 18, 19
Wikimedia Commons: Public Domain p. 5

All other images by Shutterstock

HUDSON PUBLIC LIBRARY
WOOD SQUARE
HUDSON, MA 01749

Library and Archives Canada Cataloguing in Publication

Kopp, Megan, author
    Be the change for the environment / Megan Kopp.

(Be the change)
Includes index.
Issued in print and electronic formats.
ISBN 978-0-7787-0620-5 (bound).--ISBN 978-0-7787-0632-8 (pbk.).--
ISBN 978-1-4271-7608-0 (pdf).--ISBN 978-1-4271-7604-2 (html)

    1. Human ecology--Juvenile literature. 2. Nature--Effect of
human beings on--Juvenile literature. 3. Environmental protection--
Juvenile literature. I. Title.

GF48.K56 2014   j304.2   C2014-903836-4
                                       C2014-903837-2

Library of Congress Cataloging-in-Publication Data

Kopp, Megan.
    Be the change for the environment / Megan Kopp.
       pages cm. -- (Be the change!)
    Includes index.
    ISBN 978-0-7787-0620-5 (reinforced library binding) -- ISBN 978-0-7787-0632-8 (pbk
-- ISBN 978-1-4271-7608-0 (electronic pdf) -- ISBN 978-1-4271-7604-2 (electronic htm
    1. Environmentalism--Juvenile literature. 2. Children and the environment--Juveni
literature. 3. Social action--Juvenile literature. I. Title.

    GE195.5.K67 2015
    363.7--dc23

                               2014032612

Crabtree Publishing Company

www.crabtreebooks.com   1-800-387-7650

Printed in Canada/102014/EF20140925

Copyright © **2015 CRABTREE PUBLISHING COMPANY.** All rights reserved. No part of this publication may be reproduced, stored in a retrieval system or be transmitted in any form or by any means, electronic, mechanical, photocopying, recording, or otherwise, without the prior written permission of Crabtree Publishing Company. In Canada: We acknowledge the financial support of the Government of Canada through the Canada Book Fund for our publishing activities.

Published in Canada
Crabtree Publishing
616 Welland Ave.
St. Catharines, Ontario
L2M 5V6

Published in the United States
Crabtree Publishing
PMB 59051
350 Fifth Avenue, 59th Floor
New York, New York 10118

Published in the United Kingdom
Crabtree Publishing
Maritime House
Basin Road North, Hove
BN41 1WR

Published in Australia
Crabtree Publishing
3 Charles Street
Coburg North
VIC 3058

Contents

Be the change

Some people are great leaders. Mahatma Gandhi was one of those people. Gandhi saw people not being treated fairly. He knew that was wrong. Gandhi stood up for others in peaceful ways. He believed he could make the world a better place. Some people believe Gandhi said: "Be the change you wish to see in the world."

MAKING CHANGE HAPPEN!

Gandhi's beliefs are still important to people. What do the words "be the change" mean to you?

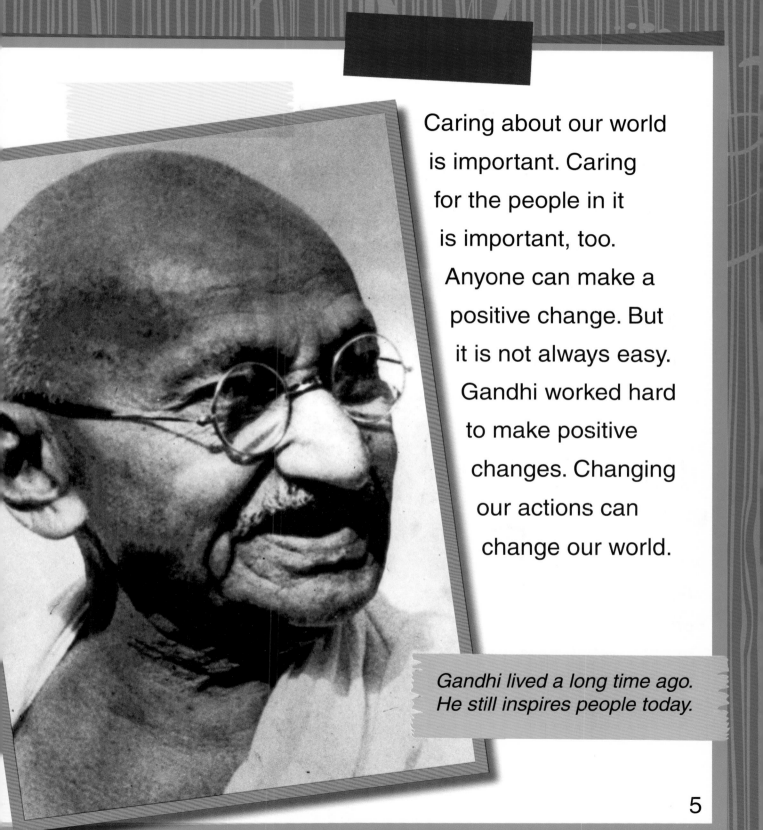

Caring about our world is important. Caring for the people in it is important, too. Anyone can make a positive change. But it is not always easy. Gandhi worked hard to make positive changes. Changing our actions can change our world.

Gandhi lived a long time ago. He still inspires people today.

The environment

Caring for Earth is everyone's job. You can be the change for the **environment**! The environment is made up of all living and non-living things. The environment includes air, land, animals, plants, and bodies of water. It gives us food, water, and air. The environment gives us everything we need to be healthy. Harming the environment can be harmful to us and other living things.

Buy in bulk to reduce on packaging.

Stewardship is the job of caring for something. Environmental stewardship means protecting and caring for our surroundings. We do this in many different ways. We can keep Earth clean by reducing our **waste**. Waste is anything you throw out. It often ends up in **landfills**. Waste can **pollute** the soil, air, and water. Try to use only what you need. That reduces waste and helps keep our environment clean.

Instead of plastic bottles, use a refillable water bottle.

Start a compost pile to reuse your leftover fruit and vegetable scraps as new soil!

7

Write on!

You are never too young to make a change to help the environment! Brooklyn Wright was only seven years old when she wrote a book. She wanted to teach others to care for the environment.

NAME:
Brooklyn Wright

FROM:
Atlanta, Georgia

CAUSE:
Putting an end to litter

iDEA

Brooklyn has won many awards for making a difference.

Change in action

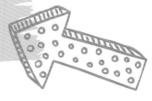

Brooklyn Wright saw litter everywhere. It was in the park, on the street, and in her schoolyard. Brooklyn knew litter was bad for the environment. She wanted to do something to help solve the problem. In second grade, Brooklyn wrote a book called *The Adventures of the Earth Saver Girl, Don't Be a Litterbug*. Earth Saver Girl is a superhero. She is on a mission to clean up litter. Brooklyn shares her book and its message with other kids. She has visited more than 300 schools and libraries. She plans to write more books on protecting animals, reducing waste, and gardening.

The environment needs superheroes!

Creating change

Brooklyn Wright found a way to change something that was important to her. She wrote a book about litter. Ideas for your change can come from many places, for example:

• reading a book

• hearing something on the radio or TV

• a lesson in school

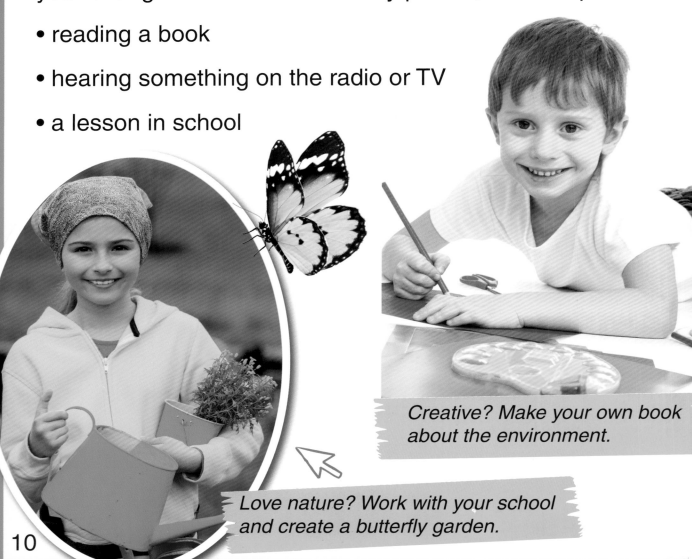

Creative? Make your own book about the environment.

Love nature? Work with your school and create a butterfly garden.

What can you do?

You can use your own skills and interests to help make a positive change!

Like being active? Join a walk-a-thon to raise money for a cause.

Enjoy teaching others? Start an **eco-club** at your school.

MAKING CHANGE HAPPEN!

What are your skills and interests? Make a list. Brainstorm ways to use these skills. How can you use your skills to help the environment?

Learning and planning

You can be the change in your environment. Find a problem that harms the environment. It should be something you care about. Learn everything you can about it. Find ways to solve the problem. Read books. **Research** on the Internet. Talk to people. For example, you can ask an adult to help you contact experts. These people work for environmental **organizations**.

Caring for Earth is like problem solving. There are problems for which you need to find solutions. Ask questions to help you solve the problem. The **action** you take to solve the problem is your **project**.

MAKING CHANGE HAPPEN!

What problem do you want to help solve?
What can you do?

12

Jessica made a list of questions for learning about her cause:

What is the problem I want to help solve? There is too much paper and plastic in recycling bins.

Who am I helping? Earth and everyone on it.

Why is this important to me? My brother told me about **precycling**. He said it cuts down waste. I thinks people would precycle if they knew how easy it was.

What can I do? I will make posters on recycled paper. These posters will teach people about precycling.

Be a Pro at Precycling!
Think before you buy!

- Bring reusable bags with you to the store.
- Do not buy items you can only use once.
- Look for packaging that can be reused or recycled.

13

Action plan

Now that you know the change you want to make, write an **action plan**. An action plan is a guide that helps you reach your goal. Your goal is what you want to accomplish. Goals can be helpful to measure the success of your action plan.

What is the goal of your action plan?

Jared's action plan

Jared wrote this action plan for his project.

Project Name: Bank on Trees

When: April 26

Goal: To replace trees taken away last year by the big flood along Meander Creek, from the wooden bridge to the underpass

Team Members: Me, my family, my friend Emily Smith and her family, and Ben Juarez and his family

Where will you get the trees? I will ask local tree farms to donate trees

How long will it take to organize? One month before planting day.

Set goal for how many trees to plant: 25 trees

Do it!

Now it's time to be the change! Jared worked hard to plan a tree planting day at Meander Creek.

April 1 Go with Dad to town office for tree-planting permit.

April 4 Visit the Juarez tree farm and pick out 25 trees for the project.

Tree farm

April 5 Visit Mr. Smith's tool rental store. Ask to borrow ten shovels and two post-hole diggers.

April 25 Go with Mom to pick up tools.

April 26 Meet everyone at the creek. Flag places to plant each tree. Dig holes and plant trees.

Don't give up

Sometimes, making a change takes time. Be patient. Things do not always happen as planned. For example, what if it rains on your action day? Be prepared! Have a rain date planned ahead of time. Be sure to let people know about the new date.

MAKING CHANGE HAPPEN!

Who will you talk to about your project? Who can help you?

Share it!

Let others know about what you have done. Be proud of what you have accomplished. Share what you have learned with your school. Spread the word to other schools. Share it with your family, neighbors, and local government. Invite others to join in. Keep your project going.

Jared made this list for sharing the success of his project:

Sharing news about your change can inspire others. **Be the change!**

- Draw pictures of my project and post on community bulletin boards

- Write a story about Making Meander Creek Happy and share with students in my school

- Make a presentation to my mom's service club about how many trees were planted

- With my parent's permission, talk to the local newspaper

Think about it!

Congratulations! You did it! You made a change. Now take a moment. Think about what you have done. This is important. It helps you realize the value of your efforts. Ask yourself questions such as:

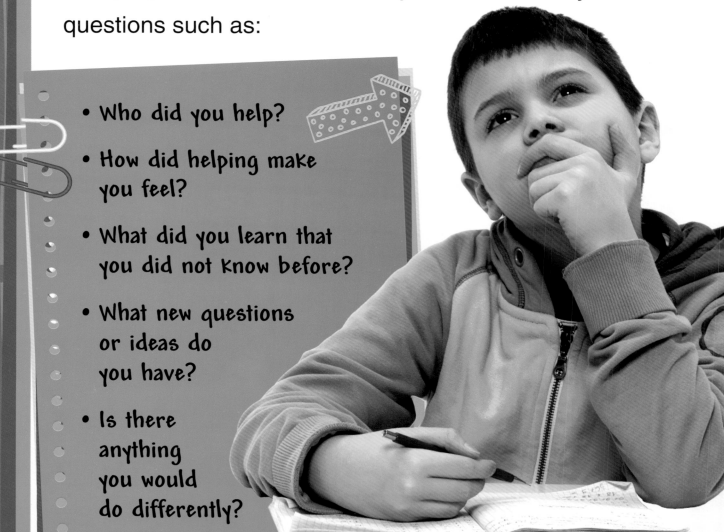

- Who did you help?

- How did helping make you feel?

- What did you learn that you did not know before?

- What new questions or ideas do you have?

- Is there anything you would do differently?

Keep being the change. Ask yourself: what are other ways to be the change? Try to do one thing each day to inspire change.

MAKING CHANGE HAPPEN!

How will you continue to make changes to help the environment? Will you make your cause a yearly event? Will you get other kids to join you next year?

Helping the environment helps you

You get what you give. It's true! When you help others, you get something back. It could be a good feeling, or it might be learning something new.

Helping others helps you, too. It gives you the chance to:

- try new things
- make new friends
- build up belief in yourself
- feel needed and important

- see more of your community
- get others to make a change
- know you can do anything you set your mind to!

Learning more

Websites

www.ecokids.ca An award-winning environmental education site from Earth Day Canada.

www.planetpals.com/ Planet Pals teaches kids about their world and how to care for it.

http://meetthegreens.pbskids.org/who/ The Greens is an animated site from PBS with videos and games about looking after the planet.

www.c2es.org/science-impacts/basics/kids This website teaches about climate change and using energy wisely.

www.earthsavergirl.com/meetbrooklyn/brooklyn.html Brooklyn Wright's website teaching kids how to help the environment.

http://climatekids.nasa.gov/butterfly-garden/ How to plant a butterfly garden.

Volunteer organizations

www.worldwildlife.org/ World Wildlife Fund raises money to support the conservation movement around the world.

www.earthday.org Earth Day Network educates and motivates people to act to ensure a healthy future for our world.

www.kidsforsavingearth.org/ Kids for Saving Earth is designed to educate, inspire, and empower children to protect the Earth's environment.

Books

Barnham, Kay. *Protect Nature*. Crabtree Publishing, 2007

Bouler, Olivia. *Olivia's Birds: Saving the Gulf*. Sterling, 2011

Dr. Seuss. *The Lorax*. Random House Books for Young Readers, 1971

Halfman, Janet. *Fur and Feathers*. Sylvan Dell Publishing, 2010

Silverstein, Shel. *The Giving Tree*. Harper Collins, 1964

Words to know

Note: Some **boldfaced** words are defined where they appear in the book.

action (AK-shuhn) noun Something that you do

action plan (AK-shuhn plan) noun The actions needed to reach your goal

cause (KAWZ) noun A goal to which people commit themselves and for which they work

eco-club (EE-ko-kluhb) noun A group who learns about environmental problems and works to solve them

environment (en-VYE-ruhn-mhnt) noun The natural surroundings of living things

landfills (LAND-filz) noun Where waste is buried under layers of earth

litter (LIT-ur) noun Pieces of garbage scattered around

organizations (or-guh-ni-ZAY-shuhns) noun Groups of people brought together for a particular purpose

pollute (PUH-loot) verb To contaminate the environment

precycling (PREE-sye-kuhl-ing) noun Reducing waste by using your own bags and buying unpackaged, reusable, or recycleable products

research (REE-surch) verb To collect information about a subject

service (SUR-vis) noun Work that helps others

A noun is a person, place, or thing. A verb is an action word that tells you what someone or something does.

Index